EXPLORE, CREATE,

Resinate

Mixed Media Techniques using ICE Resin®

JEN CUSHMAN

Book Design: Dawn DeVries Sokol
Editor/Photographer: Jen Cushman
Step-Out Photos Photographer: Carol LaValley
Copy Editor: Cheri Lenart Cann

Printed in the United States of America
Josten's Printing, Visalia, California
Contact: Mike McCoy: 888.897.9693 or emailmcoym@uplink.net

ISBN-10 0-9832239-0-4
ISBN-13 9780983223900

Dedication

This book truly wouldn't have been possible without the love and support of Susan Lenart Kazmer, my friend, business partner and my jewelry-making muse and mentor. To my husband, Greg, for always supporting whatever crazy ideas I dream up. I promised you our life together will never be boring, and for 18 years, I've kept my promise. To my beautiful children, Ty and Izabella, for teaching me that even though words are my talent and art is my passion that being a mother is the most fulfilling, humbling and time consuming job I will ever have in this lifetime.

ACKNOWLEDGMENTS

I couldn't be who I am nor do what I do without the encouragement and hands-on help of my "Village People." To my sister, Patti, for her wisdom and gift of symbolic sight and my parents, Marge and Bud, for telling me to "use my words." To my dear mother-in-law, Kay, and my babysitter Debbie Dahn for taking such good care of my busy, busy baby girl as I created the art and wrote this book. To my girlfriends Diane Roeder and Tina O'Neil for entertaining my son during back-to-back deadlines. To my sweet friend Carol LaValley for doing a brilliant job shooting my step-out photos. To the talented Dawn DeVries Sokol for rockin' the graphics and design. Last, but not least, to the ICE Resin Susan Lenart Kazmer Creative Team for your vigilant support and mad skills. I'm in awe of your beautiful work.

About the Author

JEN CUSHMAN is a natural storyteller who found mixed media art a decade ago and never looked back. She is drawn to the imperfect, the funky, the quirky, the artsy and the authentic: be it people or objects or art.

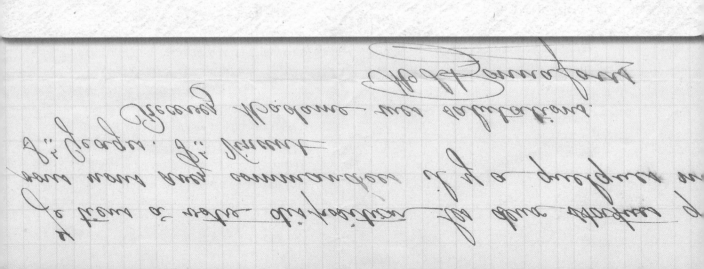

Her art has been published in *Belle Armoire Jewelry*, *Jewelry Affaire*, *Cloth Paper Scissors* 2010 Gifts Issue, *WireWork* magazine and the Crafts Channel of Lifetime Television's interactive website. As a writer/editor specializing in the visual arts, Jen has written for many national magazines, including *Phoenix Home and Garden*, *American Style*, *Niche*, *Southwest Art*, *The Artist's Magazine* and more. She currently writes a marketing column for artists in *Belle Armoire Jewelry* and the new website "Create Mixed Media".

An enthusiastic and supportive instructor, Jen teaches more than jewelry-making and paper crafting techniques. She encourages others to explore their authentic, creative process to create art that is real and personally meaningful. Learn more at www.jencushman.com.

Susan Lenart Kazmer

For more than 20 years, Susan Lenart Kazmer has been a professional artist, metalsmith and jeweler. She's also an internationally-known instructor who's been teaching mixed media techniques for over a decade.

Susan is the creator of ICE Resin®, the author of *Making Connections: A Handbook of Cold Joins for Jewelers and Mixed Media Artists* and two DVDs by Interweave Press, "Metalwork" and "Exploring Resin in Jewelry Making." Last summer, she debuted Industrial Chic™ by Susan Lenart Kazmer,™ a successful charm and jewelry component line exclusive to Michaels.

Susan was recently involved with the American Fine Craft Council and presented the 2006 award of "Most innovative use of the medium" from Robert Lui of *Ornament* magazine. Her work has been included in museum exhibits throughout the country, such as the Smithsonian in Washington D.C. and the Art Institute in New York. To learn more, visit www.susanlenartkazmer.com.

Unlock My Spirit (left) and Art to Wear (right),
Jen Cushman

Contents

Introduction

PAINTERS BEGIN with a blank canvas. Sculptors start with a lump of clay. Metalsmiths commence their creativity by reaching for a scrap of sheet metal. In every art form, a visionary begins with a small collection of raw material and works her magic to create a tangible work of art that launches beauty into the world.

As a self-taught mixed media artist, I begin my art making process with ICE Resin®, a jeweler's grade two-part epoxy resin that stays forever crystal clear like glass. As you will soon see, ICE Resin® is a magical elixir with of multitude of art making potential.

Like canvas or clay or metal, ICE Resin® speaks to me, whispering its desire to be transformed from an unassuming liquid into something extraordinary. For the past five years, I've been on a journey to develop my visual voice in mixed media jewelry, college and assemblage. Two years ago, my path intertwined with ICE Resin® in such a kismet way that it boggles the mind when I stop to ponder how all roads led me to this moment. I envision myself as an alchemist eager to be in my studio experimenting, playing, reviewing and discovering.

Aside from being simply mixed and poured, ICE Resin® can be colored, cast, embedded, sanded, drilled and altered. I'm convinced that whatever one can artistically dream up, this resin can morph itself into.

The finest examples of ICE Resin's transformative properties are seen in the extraordinary work of Metalsmith and Mixed Media Artist Susan Lenart Kazmer. For more than 20 years, Susan has been an inventor, explorer and creative genius in the field of mixed media jewelry and personal adornment.

A BRIEF HISTORY OF ICE RESIN® DEVELOPED BY SUSAN LENART KAZMER

During her studies at the Art Institute of Chicago, Susan pioneered the integration of fibers and found objects with traditional metalsmithing and jewelry techniques. As a contemporary builder of Talisman jewelry for more than twenty years, Susan creates one-of-a-kind pieces of personal

Memoirs of a Marionette (left) and *Stacked Paper* (below), Susan Lenart Kazmer

adornment by re-purposing found objects of modern-day culture, such as light bulbs, game pieces, typewriter keys, pencil stubs, rulers, et cetera and reinterpreting these artifacts into jewelry that is layered with spiritual and historical significance.

Entranced by the transparent effects of resin and its ability to allow her to incorporate ad-ditional layers of meaning into her work, Susan began experimenting with resins more than a decade ago. There were only a few products com-mercially available at the time. It concerned her to work with chemical compounds considered toxic,

The Opera Singer, Susan Lenart Kazmer

so she began investigating and researching all she could about the various types of resins on the market. This led Susan to develop her signature product, ICE Resin®, a non toxic jeweler's grade two part epoxy resin that's self-doming, self-leveling and will not fade or yellow over time.

Susan has put thousands and thousands of hours into her work with ICE Resin® as an internationally-known artist and instructor. She's the inventor and originator of the techniques in this book, including casting resin for use in jewelry, coloring it with kitchen spices, using it on delicate objects (such as quail's eggs), pouring it in layers to create dimensional collage, applying it to paper to make a translucent and waterproof art material, as well as many more interesting and groundbreaking applications.

My personal journey with ICE Resin® and Susan Lenart Kazmer began in 2005 when I was writing an art column for a well-loved, but now defunct magazine. I asked artists for recommendations of others who were blazing a trail in the field of mixed media, and Susan's name was repeatedly given to me as a person to watch.

When I saw her work, I knew I was seeing a genuine style that was so different from much of the art I examined as a visual arts writer and editor. The moment I met Susan, I realized her work is an authentic expression of her as a person, which is one of the reasons it's so extraordinary. We cultivated a friendship over the years, and I've been learning from her ever since.

The first class I took from Susan five years ago was creating transparent layers using resin. I was hooked from the moment I stirred my first mixing cup and, a few hours later, held in my hand a collaged pendant. I ordered resin and incorporated it into my mixed media art projects.

The Spring of 2009, Susan asked me to join her company as her Director of Education and Marketing. I agreed, and we developed a plan to get ICE Resin® into the hands of creative people on a grand scale.

We handpicked five artists to to create jewelry using ICE Resin and Susan's handcrafted bezels, started a blog and began publishing the results. In the past 2 years, I've thrown myself into working with resin with wild abandon, creating many of the new pieces you see in this book.

Explore, Create, Resinate: Mixed Media Techniques using ICE Resin® is another culmination of these efforts. Like the essential cookbook that you send your son or daughter off to college with, it's my hope this book is instrumental in your success to incorporate this medium into your art-making toolbox.

People often leave comments on the on the ICE Queen Zine (www.ICEResin.com) or email me directly that they're afraid to try resin because it seems too complicated or too tricky. I can assure you, there is nothing to fear. The introductory techniques in this book guarantee success. Before you know it, you may just find yourself turning your resin apprehension into an ICE Resin® addiction.

In addition to step-by-step instructions and photos, there are many tips and tricks, as well as stunning gallery pictures to delight and inspire you from myself, Susan and the Creative Team artists, all of whom are intimately familiar with the myriad of ways to achieve stunning mixed media results with ICE Resin.

So, let's get started. It's time for your art to *resinate* in a big way!

Steampunk Gentleman,
Jen Cushman

Chapter 1

What Makes
ICE Resin®
Unique

RESIN HAS BEEN USED in commercial applications for more than 50 years, but it's really only been within the past decade that fine artists have begun to explore its potential as an art medium. The problem, until recently, is that many resin products contain chemicals that are considered hazardous. Due to advancements in technology, the resin you're working with today is much different from its former counterparts.

ICE Resin® differs from other resin products because it's a jeweler's grade two-part epoxy resin that has some noteworthy attributes built into its chemistry, namely its doming, self-leveling and self-healing properties.

The resin prefers to create a "dome" shape when you pour it. You will see that as you drip it into a bezel, it looks like a drop of water and will naturally maintain the drop shape.

ICE Resin Part A and Part B kit

ICE Resin® is also self-leveling. In the past when working with resins, you had to spend extra time propping up your project to ensure your bezel was perfectly level before pouring. If not, it would leak or simply dry at a slant. ICE Resin's doming capabilities give it more surface tension, which also allows it to slowly spread out and self-level with a controlled pour. (All of this is in degrees, of course, as the laws of gravity definitely come into play.) As long as the table surface you are working on is level and your project is laying fairly flat, it will naturally accommodate the surface.

It's also important to mention the resin's self-healing properties. While it seems like a minor detail, this attribute is one of the most magical things about working with ICE Resin® because it's nearly impossible to mess up your work to the point of no repair. (More detail is provided on this in Chapter 9.)

ICE Resin's most significant characteristic, however, is its jeweler's grade quality. Once dry and fully cured, it's crystal clear with a beautiful glass like finish, and it will stay that way forever. Your creativity will last a lifetime, as your work will never fade, yellow or become brittle. Its surface is strong, and jewelry made with it can be comfortably worn and put through the paces of daily living. For jewelry artists who sell their work, it is this feature that sets ICE Resin® apart from others.

Now that you know what makes ICE Resin® so special, it's time to learn the basic techniques.

Summer Sunflower, Jen Cushman

Chapter 2

Mixing and Pouring

The most important thing to consider when mixing ICE Resin® is to remember that it is a two-part epoxy resin. Part A is the resin and Part B is the hardener. It works on a one-to-one ratio, meaning equal amounts of both resin and hardener must be used together. An accurate measurement is essential to success.

As you get ready to work with ICE Resin®, prepare your materials and set up your workspace. Plastic garbage bags are the most convenient and economical surface to work on. Cut open one or two bags and adhere to your work table with some low-tack painters tape or masking tape. Have baby wipes nearby to clean up any resin drops that may spill on the table or floor or get on your hands. You may choose to wear latex gloves if you wish to avoid any possible stickiness.

Have your empty bezels ready to work with, plus any inclusions (Chapter 3) nearby that you may wish to use. If you are making a mini collage for your jewelry, work out the design ahead of time and have the pieces ready to go. You have an open working time with ICE Resin® of about 45 minutes, so it helps to have your images prepped and ready before you mix.

TIP: There are many types of bezels to work with. At its most simple definition, a bezel is any object with a slight dish shape to it. Most of the handcrafted bezels at ICE Resin® Susan Lenart Kazmer (www.ICEResin.com) were made by Susan and cast in sterling silver, bronze or mixed metals for your creative use. Once you start looking, you will see a variety of found object bezels, from bottle and champagne caps to vintage hardware keyholes, old medicine tins to punched metal circles you can dome yourself with a dapping block.

MIXING

1

To begin mixing, use the plastic measuring cups provided in the kit. Begin pouring the Part A resin into a measuring cup.

2 Stop pouring when you have filled half the cup with Part A resin.

3 Add an equal amount of Part B hardener on top of the resin (use the same cup).

4 I recommend you get into the habit of pouring the resin first and then the hardener second because the resin is denser and it makes for a more accurate measurement.

5

Begin mixing the two parts together with the craft stick provided in the kit, folding the resin and hardener into each other as though you are beating an egg, rather than using a stirring action. As you mix, tiny bubbles will form and the color will turn slightly opaque. Don't worry, as ICE Resin® is chemically engineered to self-correct.

8 After about a minute of folding, your resin and hardener will begin to blend and it's fine to switch to a stirring action. Be sure to scrape down the sides of the mixing cup as your stir and ensure that you've "lifted" the resin from the bottom of the cup as you folded the two parts together. Continue mixing thoroughly for a full 2 minutes.

7 When you have mixed for 2 full minutes, set the mixed resin aside for 5 minutes to rest. This small amount of time will allow its self-leveling chemistry to work, which will help dissipate the tiny bubbles caused during mixing. This is a very important step to create crystal clear bezels. Please do not rush the process, as the small wait time yields noticeable results.

TIP: Place the mixed resin under a warm task lamp for 5 minutes, as the heat will help activate the process. If you closely watch your mixed resin during this time, you will see teeny tiny bubbles rising to the surface and popping.

POURING

1 Place your background image or object into your bezel. If the image is light, like a torn strip of paper, you may wish to adhere it to the back of your bezel with a tiny drop of craft glue to ensure it doesn't "lift" with the pour.

2 Using the same craft stick that you used for mixing, begin to slowly drip the resin into your bezel. Take your time and work in a controlled manner, dripping enough to fill your bezel just shy of its top.

To easily create a beautiful dome (rounded bubble-like top) on your bezel, it's best to pour in stages. For the first pour, stop before the liquid reaches the top and let dry. Once the bezel is dry, mix up a smaller batch of ICE Resin® and slowly drip into your bezel, watching for the natural dome effect caused by the surface tension of the resin.

TIP: The exception to this rule is when you're working with small bezels because surface pressure of the smaller bezel combined with the resin's natural drop shape creates an easy dome in one pour.

3 Do not move your bezel after pouring. Let your project sit, but check on its progress about 30 minutes after finishing the pour to watch for any wayward bubbles. You can easily pop the bubbles with the end of a toothpick while the resin is still in its liquid state.

ICE Resin® works best when measured carefully, mixed thoroughly and then left alone to work its chemistry. A little bit of patience is the key to perfection.

Discard all measuring cups and craft sticks after mixing and pouring. They should not be reused so as to not contaminate a fresh batch of mixed resin.

TIP: ICE Resin® now comes in a 1-ounce size with a two-part plunger delivery system that's taken the measuring out of the equation. With your thumbs, place equal pressure on both plungers and squeeze into a mixing cup. Mix and pour. You can fill 10 deep-welled bezels with the 1-ounce size. The best part about the new delivery system is that you can mix a small amount for one or two bezels and save the rest.

TIP: Go ahead and design an additional bezel or two when creating your artwork. That way, you can use up any extra mixed resin you may have in your cup rather than wasting it.

POURING AN UNEVEN SURFACE

1 Sometimes your bezels do not lay perfectly flat, particularly if you are using pre-made ring blanks or bracelet cuffs. A simple way to fashion a level surface is to cut a slit into your inexpensive sponges.

2 Nestle your bezel into the slit in the sponge and push down slightly to secure.

3 Drip resin into your bezel, stopping just shy of the top. Leave the bezel resting inside the sponge until dry.

DRYING AND CURING

Students always ask about the drying time for ICE Resin®. It doesn't matter if you're pouring a small shallow bezel, a deep welled bezel, a large mold or creating a piece of resin paper, the drying time is the same. As long as it's measured carefully and mixed thoroughly, ICE Resin® takes about six hours to dry. If the room is on the cooler or more humid side, it can take up to 10 hours to fully dry.

Once dry, it will feel completely smooth to the touch, like glass, and will look crystal clear. You can work with your bezels or resin paper (Chapter 7) as soon as they are dry to the touch.

It takes 3 days to cure, but this just means that you won't want to put your newly-made pieces in an airtight container because a lack of oxygen while the resin is curing could cause your pieces to turn cloudy. Once the resin is fully cured, it will be rock hard and crystal clear forever.

You'll want to use your ICE Resin® kit within one year of purchasing. While unopened bottles have an indefinite shelf life, once you open your bottles, air will slowly affect the hardener over time, causing it to turn darker yellow in color. If your hardener has yellowed, don't worry, it's most likely still good. To be safe, pour a test bezel or a practice piece of paper before tackling a large or important project.

Some craft resins/hardeners have added chemistry to prolong their shelf life, which can make the difference between products containing potentially harmful chemicals and those without. According to the Materials Safety Data Sheet (MSDA) of ICE Resin® both part A resin and part B hardener contain no hazardous ingredients.

MORE TIPS AND TRICKS:

❏ In the past when working with resins, it was common to add a little bit more hardener to the resin to ensure proper drying and curing. This is not necessary with ICE Resin®. An accurate one-to-one measurement is best.

❏ Resin can be affected by the ambient temperature and humidity in a room. Nothing terrible will happen if the room is too hot or humid or cold, except that these factors could affect how easily the resin mixes, how well the bubbles dissipate and how quickly your projects dry.

❏ If you are working with resin in the winter and the house/studio is a bit cold, it helps to first warm up your bottles of Part A resin and Part B hardener in a pan of hot tap water and let them sit for about 40 minutes before measuring. This will help its self-leveling chemistry activate so the tiny bubbles dissipate as they should. Never put your resin in a microwave to heat up.

❏ Do not allow your resin kit to freeze. Ice crystals can change its chemical composition. Fortunately, you can fix this by warming the bottles in hot tap water for about 45 minutes. Without first warming it, your once-frozen resin will mix and pour thickly and may dry cloudy. Store your resin alongside your other craft products in your home or studio to prevent freezing.

❏ People who've worked with craft resins in the past have found tricks to get around its finicky quirks—mainly persistent bubbles. ICE Resin® is a new kind of resin with enhanced technology. It's not necessary to wave a flame over it after pouring, or attempt to place direct heat on it by using an embossing heat gun or hairdryer. If you wish to introduce heat to speed up drying time, the safest and most consistent method is to place your resin bezels under a warm task lamp for the first hour or two after your pour. For safety's sake, keep the light bulb six to 10 inches from your bezels. This is an effective method during the winter months when room temperatures are cooler.

be true

If Only
Kristen Robinson

Pearl of Wisdom
Kristen Robinson

Au Revoir

Jèn Cushman

Let Nature Lead the Way, Jen Cushman

Chapter 3

EMBEDDING AND INCLUSIONS

YOU WILL MOST LIKELY ALWAYS be embedding some type of image or object into your ICE Resin® projects. While it's a simple process to do so, there are some tips and tricks that will make working with resin much more enjoyable.

One of the things I see when teaching ICE Resin® classes is that students get so excited about this amazing new art material that they want to jump right in and immediately try to replicate some of the more advanced inspirational designs by Susan, myself or the working artists who are part of the Creative Team. While I love students' enthusiasm, I would be remiss if I didn't encourage them to learn the basics and work their way toward advanced techniques.

In nearly every instance that I've needed to help someone troubleshoot mistakes, most are caused by the person not reading the

directions as thoroughly as they should have, or simply being too eager to wade through the fundamentals. Here are the beginning steps for adding images, snips of paper or small objects into your bezels during a resin pour.

1 Begin as described in Chapter 3 by working out your design ideas first and placing them into your bezel as a dry test run before mixing up your ICE Resin®.

When working with photographs or images you wish to remain colorfast (looking exactly as is on your printed images or pictures), you must first seal them to create a coating between the resin and the images. (More on sealing images in the next chapter.)

2 Mix ICE Resin® as explained in Chapter 2. If you want your background paper or image to stay firmly attached to the back of the bezel, apply a small dot of craft glue to the image and place it into the bezel. Begin dripping resin into your bezel, stopping when you've filled one-third to one-half way from the top.

TRICK: When embedding, drip enough resin into your bezel to create a nice bottom layer (usually one-third to one-half way from the top depending on the number of inclusions) and then add your objects. The weight of the object when added to the liquid will raise the level of the resin slightly, which could cause it to spill over if you've already filled your bezel to the top. It's always easier to add more resin than it is to get rid of overflows later.

3

Using your craft stick, apply a thin layer of resin to the back of the next image/inclusion you wish to embed. This will help create a liquid seal that will fuse with your poured resin when adding your object. Most bubbles that remain after the resin dries are caused during the embedding stage when you introduce air to the already poured resin as you add your inclusions. Applying a thin layer of resin first to your objects will help counteract air bubbles.

4 Slowly sink your image or object into your bezel using your fingers or tweezers. You can adjust the position with the tip of a toothpick, gently pushing your inclusion into place.

TRICK: If you are pouring into a square or rectangle bezel, use the tip of your toothpick to work resin into the corners.

You can stop here or continue to add more inclusions using these techniques. After embedding images/text/objects, continue dripping mixed resin into the bezel until it is filled just shy of its top.

5

TIP: To create a beautiful dome on your bezels, it's best to work in stages. It's easier to mix a small amount of fresh resin and add the dome in a second pour than it is to overfill your bezels the first time and have to clean them up later.

Set your work aside to dry, but check on it again after 30 minutes to see if any additional air trapped during the embedding process created bubbles that have risen to the surface but won't dissipate without your intervention. Pop with a toothpick. If you've waited too long and your resin is already setting up and turning thick, you may have to wait until your piece dries to fix it. (See Chapter 9 for fixes).

Just about anything can be embedded in ICE Resin® from paper, metal, charms, beads, buttons, gears, watch parts, sand, fabric, ribbon, pebbles, dried flowers, candy, bones, wings, feathers, wood, sticks, eggs, leaves, et cetera. All materials, particularly organic ones, must be completely dry when using them with resin.

8 You don't always have to use text or images with your resin. It can be fun to experiment with your inclusions by adding textural items.

9 I was recently inspired by a winter night sky filled with stars. I tried to re-create the feeling with some blue glass beads and star charms in a stylish mixed metal bezel.

A Summer's Picnic
Kecia Deveney

Madame

les deux statues g

il y a quelques n

Coin of the Realm
Jane Salley

truth

Truth
Kristen Robinson

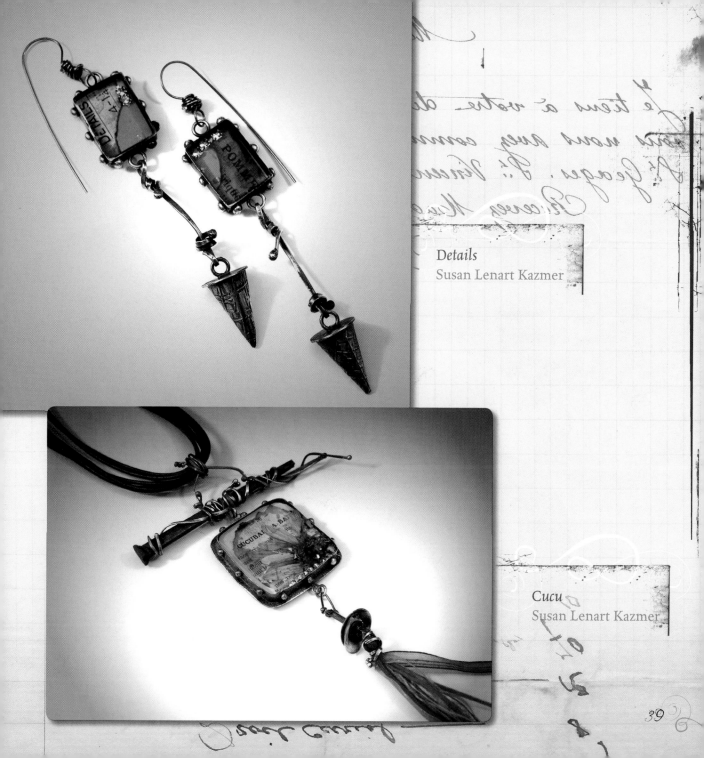

Details
Susan Lenart Kazmer

Cucu
Susan Lenart Kazmer

Baby Love, Jen Cushman

Chapter 4

Using Photographs
AND SEALING
IMAGES

WHEN WORKING WITH PHOTOGRAPHS or images you wish to remain colorfast (looking exactly as is on your printed images or pictures), you must first seal them to create a coating between the resin and the images. You can seal in a variety of ways.

If the images are color copies or laser printed with dry ink, you can paint a light coating of Collage Pauge™ or gel medium onto them with a paintbrush and allow to dry. You can also seal them with a quick spray of a clear coat lacquer craft product.

For images printed directly from your inkjet printer, you can use a light spray coat sealer and let dry, but my preferred method is to encase images in either packing tape or clear contact paper (the kind you buy as shelf liner paper with a clear side on one side and a sticky side on the other). I have a few reasons for this. I find it not only to be the quickest method, but there's also little chance of the ink smearing and running.

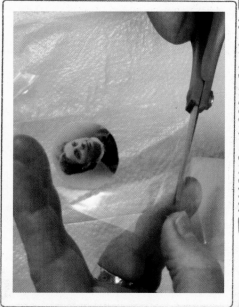

If using a piece of packing tape or clear contact paper, make a little art sandwich with your image, sealing both the front and the back.

Cut around the image with scissors, leaving the tiniest of sealed edge to ensure resin doesn't seep seep in between the tape. For images printed at your local copy shop or on a laser printer, it's best to use Collage Pauge or gel medium to seal your images. You shouldn't have smearing issues when using a dry ink to begin with.

4. *Once your photos and images are sealed, use them as background images for your bezels or embed them as you've learned in previous chapters.*

TIP: You don't need to seal your photos and images every time. If you like your art a little distressed to begin with, or are using vintage images, non-sealed images can often achieve a time-worn look. The best way to learn your aesthetic is to experiment with the same image and two bezels, sealing one image and leaving the other as is. You will quickly know your preference after some experimentation.

TIP: For a touch of bling, embed rhinestones or flat backed crystals onto your photos.

Swirls and Giggles
Kecia Deveney

Pearl's Dream
Kecia Deveney

End of the Spear Clasp
Deryn Mentock

Still
Deryn Mentock

Great Grandmother
Kristen Robinson

Transformation, Jen Cushman

Chapter 5

Working with
OPEN-BACKED
BEZELS

THIS IS ONE OF MY favorite techniques that Susan invented. The juxtaposition of negative and positive space is an important theme in her work. She created a line of open-backed bezels in 2003 for her students to use with resin in her classes, and these bezels are still the most popular sellers.

This technique has been published in many jewelry and mixed media magazines over the years, but it's been gaining in popularity as more and more artists and crafters discover ICE Resin®. I've incorporated open-backed bezels into my work because the combination of imagery and transparency creates a gorgeous layered collage look.

To use an open-backed bezel with ICE Resin®, you must create a barrier to keep the resin from leaking from the bezel. The easiest way to do this is to use either duct tape, packing tape or clear contact paper. My preference is clear packing tape because it provides a good seal with the least traces of texture.

1 *Prepare your workspace with trash bags, resin kit, mixing cups, toothpicks, craft stick, bezels, tape, images and inclusions. Have your design worked out and your images/paper cut to size before you mix your resin.*

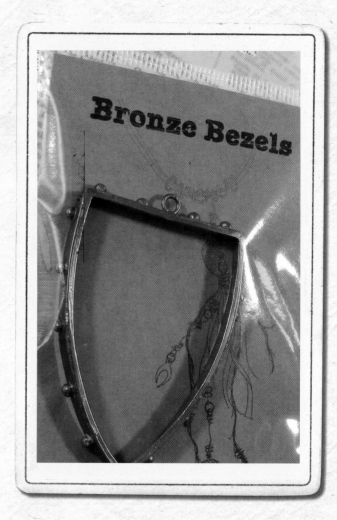

Bronze Bezels

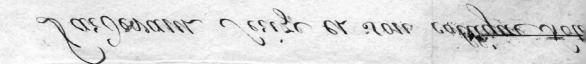

An easy way to size your image is to lay the bezel down onto your piece of paper or image and trace around it with a pencil.

3 Cut your paper slightly smaller than your tracing.

4 Ensure a comfortable fit in your bezel.

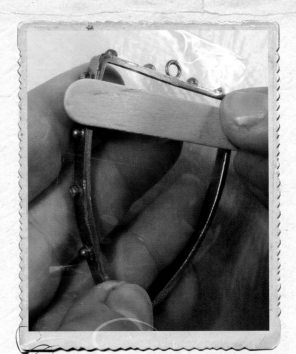

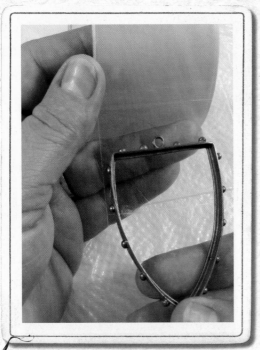

6 Fold the edges of the tape onto itself to create a smooth edge. This extra little step helps you keep your hand from sticking to the tape as you pour. Burnish the metal edges of the bezel to the sticky part of the tape with a bone folder, the back of a spoon or your craft stick that comes with the kit. You can use your fingers as long as you firmly adhere the tape to the bezel. Resin will leak unless you've created a tight seal.

5 Tear off a piece of tape and adhere the back of your open-backed bezel to the sticky side.

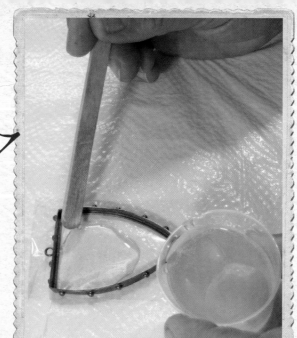

7

Place your sealed bezel right side up on the table. Mix resin according to the directions in Chapter 2 and begin to drip into the bezel, filling it about one-third of the way.

8

Using your craft stick, smear a little bit of resin onto the cut piece of background paper to create a liquid seal to diminish bubbles caused during embedding.

9

Add your pre-cut images, paper and/or inclusions.

10 Adjust cut paper background by gently using a toothpick to move paper to fit snugly inside bezel.

11 If you didn't first seal your paper, you will see the resin wicking into the paper fibers and turning the paper translucent.

12 Drip another thin layer of resin onto the paper and gently work resin into the corners of your bezel with the craft stick. This will also help any bubbles to work their way to the surface.

13 Remember that if you are adding a large inclusion (such as the butterfly wing shown here), it's best to coat a thin layer of resin onto the object before embedding to keep from introducing too much air.

14

Slowly drip more resin on top of and around the inclusion.

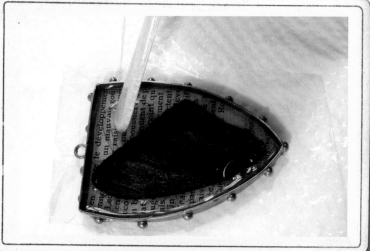

15 If you are layering inclusions (such as the metal saying here), coat the front and back of additional objects with a thin layer of resin before embedding. Watch for bubbles as you embed, and pop with the tip of a toothpick.

16 Continue to slowly drip more resin until your bezel is filled just shy of its top. With a large bezel, such as this shield shape, it's best to let your first pour fully dry and then mix up more resin to create a dome shape with a second layer.

17

Do not move your bezels after you've poured them. When your work is dry to the touch and feels smooth like glass, remove the tape backing by peeling it off. The open-backed bezel will have a lovely translucency to it when the light shines through it.

TIP: It helps to check the corner of the bezel first. If the resin is still a little tacky on the back, set aside longer to fully dry.

Sometimes the tape will leave a sticky residue on the back of the bezel. You can use a small amount of Goo-Gone™ or un du® on a paper towel to remove after the resin is fully dry.

TIP: Inexpensive packing tapes, like those from a dollar store, seem to leave much more glue residue on open-backed bezels than the name brand packing tapes do. For this reason, I spend the extra money on the tape I use for my resin work.

TRICK: Sometimes the back of your bezel is not completely smooth because it picked up the slight texture of the tape. For a crystal clear look, you can gently knock down the resin with a piece of fine grit sandpaper and then re-seal the back with a thin layer of freshly-mixed resin "painted" on with an inexpensive plastic paintbrush.

He Loves Me
Jen Cushman

The Girl in the
Violet Ball Gown
Barbe Saint John

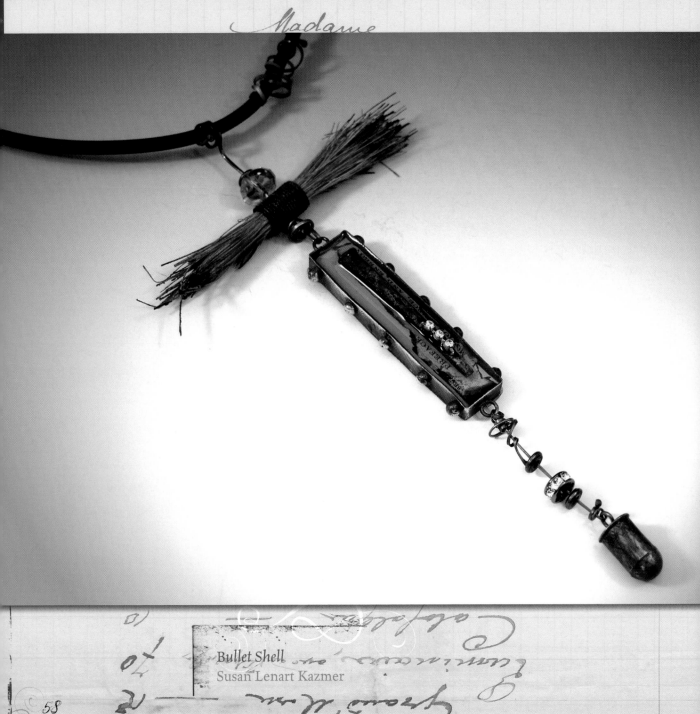

Bullet Shell
Susan Lenart Kazmer

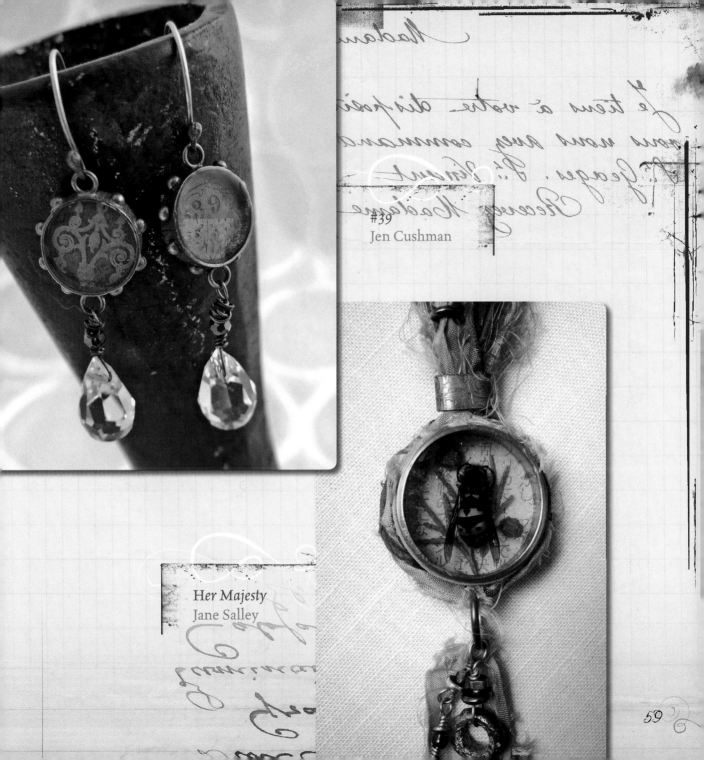

#39
Jen Cushman

Her Majesty
Jane Salley

Copper and Gold, Jen Cushman

Chapter 6

ADDING COLOR

THERE ARE COLORANTS on the market for use with craft resins, but Susan discovered when developing ICE Resin® that natural materials work best and are the easiest to keep handy in the studio. When she first looked into coloring resin, her fine art training led her to use artist quality oil paint. It's still the preferred method for adding pigment.

She also developed the techniques of using dry pigment powders and common kitchen spices to add color and texture to her resin artwork.

One of my favorite materials to work with is colored mica powders. Perfect Pearls™ by Ranger® have a resin-binder built into them and work beautifully with ICE Resin®.

To add color, mix resin as explained in the previous chapters. The time to add pigment is after your resin is thoroughly mixed, but before you pour.

1 *Using the tip of a toothpick, scrape a miniscule amount of oil paint directly from its tube and mix into the same measuring cup as the already mixed resin.*

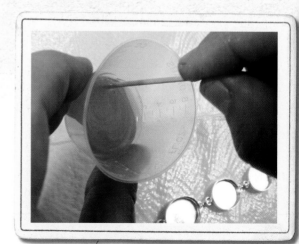

2 *Swirl the toothpick around into the resin to release the color and then continue mixing using your craft stick.*

TIP: Remember the kindergarten saying when adding color to your resin: A drop is a lot.

TIP: If your oil paints are a little old or dried out, take a drop out with the tip of your toothpick and mix the paint thoroughly on a plastic plate or lid first. Old paint can cause flakes in your resin.

3 Adding two colors to your ICE Resin® can create a cool effect when you wish to experiment artistically. This is a more advanced technique, so be sure to experiment with custom mixing your colors after you get a good feel for the basic technique.

4 Allow your mixed resin to rest for an additional 5 minutes and then pour your colored resin into your bezels or craft molds. You can embed images/text/objects and work with your colored resin just as you would if it were clear.

TIP: You can add surface treatments to your colored bezels after they dry, like stamping images onto the surface (like I did with this colored resin bracelet). Be sure to use a solvent-based ink, such as StāzOn®. The colored ink in dye-based inks can "lift" into the resin or cause a slight smearing if not completely dry. If using dye ink, quickly heat set the ink with a craft heat gun. After stamping, be sure to "seal" with a thin coat of resin to keep the stamped images from rubbing off over time.

TRICK: One of the most wonderful attributes of ICE Resin® is its glasslike appearance. I enjoy adding spots of color to my bezels with glitter, colored mica flakes or tiny bits of gold and silver leaf after I pour my bezels. Mica powders can be swirled into resin with a tip of a toothpick for some interesting effects.

PRE-MADE CRAFT MOLDS

There are a number of jewelry making craft molds available that allow you to create resin cabochons, which are especially pretty when you color your resin. You can use these molds with ICE Resin® the same way you would use bezels.

> **TIP:** Many of the molds are made of a firmer plastic, which will require you to use a mold release agent to ensure easy removal of your dried pieces. If you don't have mold release spray, you can use a dab of olive oil in a pinch. Just apply a drop of olive oil onto a piece of paper towel and coat the inside of your mold before pouring resin.

Measure and mix ICE Resin® thoroughly. Add color to your resin in the mixing cup and stir until the color is even throughout. When working with glitter, I find it easier to mix it up in the measuring cup before pouring. Fine glitter is so light that it has a tendency to "lift" or rise to the surface when sprinkled directly into the molds or bezels.

After you've learned the basics and begin to explore advanced techniques, color is one of the areas where you can take your resin work to incredible new levels.

La Luna
Jen Cushman

Frequently Asked Question: Can you color ICE Resin® with acrylic paint? Yes, and you can also use alcohol inks, dye ink re-inkers, et cetera. The reason for the preference is because oil paint and resin are naturally oil-based products and it's best to keep similar materials together for optimal quality.

My Dad's Love
Kecia Deveney

Little Egypt
Barbe Saint John

Green Eyed Gems
Susan Lenart Kazmer

Christmas Flower,
Jen Cushman

Chapter 7

MAKING RESIN PAPER

HUMANKIND HAS BEEN BEGUILED by paper for centuries. From early Egyptian papyrus, to Medieval Monks painstakingly copying ancient religious teachings into handmade books, to the modern printing press; the written word on paper is often seen as the genesis of Human intelligence. Ever since people first learned to read and write, there are those born with the visual acumen to see paper as more than a book or a writing tablet. These artists see paper as an art medium, the raw material of unfettered creativity.

I have to admit it was Susan's resin paper technique that really got my creative juices stewing. I saw so much paper crafting potential that my mind's eye nearly swooned.

Susan first developed the idea of applying resin to paper in 2000 when she began making larger art journals incorporating her metal-and-fiber attachment techniques. The idea of incorporating transparent text into her work was, and still is, avant-garde.

I've been experimenting with ICE Resin® and every type of paper I can lay my hands on. I've used stamps, image transfers, paints, inks, dyes, pigment powders, watercolors, masks, resists, and just about every kind of mixed media technique I've learned over the years and then took it a step further by applying resin. There is an alchemy that occurs when ICE Resin® wicks into paper fibers. I find it magical.

The technique itself is quite simple. The real artistry comes from what you do with it.

To make resin paper, have all your supplies ready and at your work table. You need an ICE Resin® kit, paper, plastic garbage bags, inexpensive sponges, latex gloves, baby wipes and lots of open work space.

Gather papers to resin. If you wish to do surface treatments, such as stamping, painting or inking, complete this step before doing your resin pour. You can add stamps or paint later but you may wish to re-seal, and I find my paper to be less flexible when resin is thickly applied.

Cut open your garbage bags and tape them to your work table with a low tack painters tape or making tape. The oil coating in the garbage bags will keep your paper from sticking to its surface as it dries.

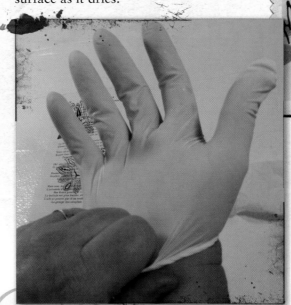

1. Put latex gloves on your hands to keep them from getting sticky as you apply resin to paper.

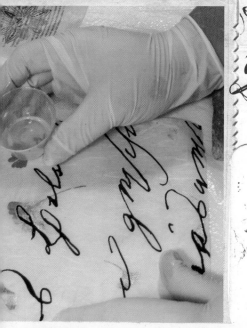

Lay your papers onto the garbage bags and mix up a full mixing cup (1 ounce) of ICE Resin® as you've learned in previous chapters.

TRICK: Paper loves resin and will quickly seep into its fibers. It takes much more resin to create resin paper than it does when simply pouring bezels. To save time, you can measure and pour multiple cups of ICE Resin® and put them aside until you're ready to use them. As long as you do not mix Part A resin and Part B hardener and activate the chemistry, the two ingredients can sit inertly next to each other for hours. See image number 4 in the mixing section of Chapter 2 for a visual.

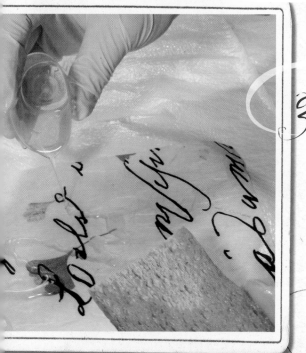

Go slow and pour a small amount of resin onto your paper. You can also dip an inexpensive sponge that's been cut into smaller pieces into the resin and begin to apply it to the paper in a gentle wiping motion. It's best to begin in the center of the paper and work your way toward the edges. Keep your application thin.

4 Within seconds of wiping on the resin you will see the paper begin to darken and turn more translucent. This is good.

Continue to cover the paper with resin. When finished with one side, flip the paper over and do the same to the back side. Keep the application thin, but use enough resin to fully cover the paper. You can tell when you need to add more resin becquse there will be opaque spots in the paper where the resin hasn't seeped into the fibers yet.

5

TIP: Whichever side you wish to use in your artwork is the side that should dry facing up. The paper will pick up the slight texture on the garbage bags. If you wish to ensure both sides are perfectly smooth, you'll need to apply to one side and let completely dry. Then mix up a new batch and do the other side.

Leave the resin coated paper to dry. Because you're wiping on a thin coat of resin with a sponge, there are no bubbles to worry about.

The paper should dry in 6 to 10 hours and feel dry to the touch. It will have a smooth feel, like plastic coating. When dry, grab a corner and gently pull from the plastic garbage bag. It will easily release.

TIP: You can work with your paper as soon as its dry. For storage, don't stack freshly resined paper on top of each other or they may stick together as they cure. Place wax paper between the stacks before storing, or simply allow them to air dry and fully cure for 3 days before stacking.

Paper and resin is a most interesting combination. There's no telling how certain papers will react to the resin in terms of their ability to remain supple over time. I have found that new scrapbooking papers, which are acid free and lignin free can become brittle after a year. Vintage papers/ephemera and many handmade papers remain soft and flexible. I presume it has to do with the way contemporary paper is commercially made. Susan still has some of her first journals when she invented the technique a decade ago and the papers are still as crystal clear transparent and supple as the day she made them.

French Journal
Susan Lenart Kazmer

Letters to My Lover
Susan Lenart Kazmer

Winged Things
Deryn Mentock

Lipstick
Jen Cushman

Fragments of Fall
Barbe Saint John

Stacked
Susan Lenart Kazmer

After the Fall
Deryn Mentock

Vaudeville
Susan Lenart Kazmer

Grandma's Buttons, Jen Cushman

Chapter 8

QUICK AND EASY CASTING

AN ADVANCED TECHNIQUE WITH ICE Resin® is to cast with it. There are some really wonderful multi-dimensional art projects that can be made using molds and resin. Susan is a pioneer in resin casting and is known internationally for her intricate Circus Troupe Figures created from her sculpted and handmade art molds, her cast ICE Resin® body parts and elaborate costumes made from metals and found objects.

At a more basic level, casting is an easy and fun technique to make multiples from one-of-a-kind objects. I have a collection of vintage metal buttons made during the 1930s that were given to me by my maternal grandmother. This collection is precious to me, so I don't like to use the originals in my artwork. That was, of course, until I discovered how easy it is to make a mold and replicate them in resin.

There are various brands of molding putty available. Look for a two part silicone molding putty that can make simple, but detailed, molds. With most molding putty, you must work quickly, as the open working time is usually 5 minutes or less.

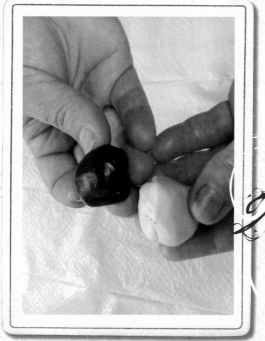

To make a mold: Have the item(s) you wish to cast ready and sitting on your work table. The object should be clean and dry. Dirt, dust, paint flakes and other debris can transfer to your mold and then to your resin if not clean.

Pinch off equal parts of A and B silicone putty and begin to blend together with your fingers. Unlike resin where you need exact measurements, you can "eyeball" the two parts, trying to keep them equal. Most putties are non toxic and food safe, so unless you have a reaction to silicone, you can work directly with your hands.

3

The two parts are always colored differently to make it easier to tell when its evenly mixed. Kneed the two parts together until the striations of color are fully blended. It's best to work quickly and mix within a minute or less.

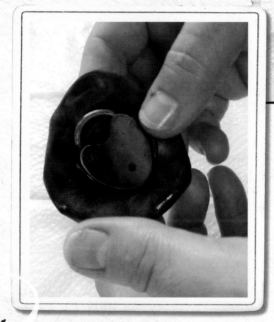

4 Immediately press your object into the ball of mixed putty, creating a tight fitting mold. The putty must be in firm contact with the original object to leave a clear impression. The open working time is usually about 5 minutes.

5 Since you'll be working with resin, be sure to construct a cup shape with the sides of your mold so it doesn't leak after pouring. Also, be sure to make the back of the mold flat so its level and resin doesn't seep out.

8 Set aside your object for about 20 minutes to dry. When the putty is fully dry, it will easily pull away from the original object. You've now created a reusable mold to cast with.

TIP: Most brands of silicone putty are flexible. You can most likely omit using a mold release spray before pouring resin when making your own custom mold.

CASTING

1 To make a cast resin piece, mix ICE Resin® according to the directions in previous chapters and slowly pour into your mold. Be careful not to add too much resin, causing it to over flow.

TRICK: If your mold doesn't sit flat, you can prop it up and level it by suspending it in a container (like the mixing cups that come with your resin kit).

2. Set aside your poured mold and let dry. When the back is dry with a glasslike finish, squeeze the ends of your mold to pop out your cast resin piece.

3. Many clear cast pieces don't look like much when they are freshly popped from their molds. You can add drama to your cast resin by rubbing paint into it and wiping off excess with a paper towel.

You may notice that sometimes your cast piece will have a lot of little bubbles just below the surface. This is caused by the tight fitting mold keeping the bubbles from working their way to the surface and dissipating. Sand the piece with a fine 600 grit sandpaper and then rub some color into the mold. This is less noticeable when the resin is colored before casting. Also, subsequent castings are much more clear than the first one.

TIP: These molds can be reused a number of times for additional castings before they begin to dry out and crack.

The Ballerina
Susan Lenart Kazmer

The Unicyclist
Susan Lenart Kazmer

Cranberry Glass
Barbe Saint John

Je tiens à vo
vous nous avez
St. Geages. St.
Recevez

Peeking Out
From The Cage
Kecia Deveney

Red Flowers
Jane Salley

The Gossamer Bat
Barbe Saint John

89

Je tiens à v...
...ous nous ave...
S.t Geages. P...
Recev...

Angel on My Wrist
Jane Salley

Cicada
Barbe Saint John

Crystal Ball
Jen Cushman

Teal², Jen Cushman

Chapter 9

Clean Up,
OVER SPILLS
AND MISTAKES

NO MATTER HOW CAREFUL you are when doing your ICE Resin® pours, there will most likely be times when you're a little heavy handed or work a little too fast. Odds are good you'll have some minor clean up when you first begin working with resin.

After that first class with Susan years ago, I eagerly poured a dozen carefully-collaged bezels at my kitchen table one evening. As I stood up, I realized the tape from where I taped the kitchen garbage bag to the table had stuck to my pants. Whoosh! All my work came crashing to the floor. What I would have given to have someone tell me what I'm about to tell you:

It's OK, really. It is practically impossible to mess up ICE Resin®. Why? Because it's jeweler's grade, self-leveling and self-healing.

I was teaching a class at a local art store where students absolutely had to take their work with them. One of the students dropped her bezel outside and came back in distress. By that time, it was already 3 hours after the pour and the resin had definitely set up. I picked the pieces of dirt and grass off the top of her bezel, used the pad of my finger to gently round out the resin and told her it would be OK.

She called the store owner the next day to say when it dried there was only a slight bump. She was amazed and sold on ICE Resin®, but she also wanted to know if there was any way to fix her bezel so it looked more perfect. I told her to sand it down with 320 grit sandpaper until the dried resin was just shy of the top of the bezel, finish off sanding with a finer 600 grit sandpaper to remove the deeper scratches, mix up a new batch and carefully pour another layer to get the dome she was looking for. *Voilá!*

Here are some techniques for clean up:

If you pour too much and it drips down the sides of your bezel, gently clean the sides with the tip of a baby wipe. (Do not use water. Resin is an oil-based product and oil-and-water doesn't mix well). Baby wipes seem to have a touch of baby oil in them which is why they work well. Set aside to dry.

Once your bezel is dry, you can use a small half-round jeweler's file to abrade off the dried resin layer. If you are working with a metal bezel, file gently as to avoid scratches in the metal. If the resin gets into the attachment loop of your bezel, use the round file to poke through the hole and gently twist to clean.

If you are concerned to touch an over poured bezel while it's wet, let it dry and then file off the excess with a jeweler's file.

If you filled much too aggressively and there's a lot of dried resin, you can snip off the excess with a pair of scissors and then file.

Alternatively, you can use a filing bit on a hand tool, like a Dremel®, to quickly remove the over poured resin.

TIP: Clean any of your spills within 3 days of your pour. Once ICE Resin® is cured, it stays rock hard and glass like and it takes lots more effort to get the spills filed off.

If your resin is still tacky after 24 hours you either did not measure carefully or mix thoroughly enough. You can mix a fresh batch of resin and add more to your bezel. If you've already "domed" your bezel, use a disposable paintbrush or the tip of a paper towel to "paint" on a new sealer coat.

If you didn't catch an aggressive bubble before the resin dried, you can use a small hand tool, like a Dremel® to drill out the bubble (be careful not to drill through the metal or so far down to the image that you mar it). You can mix more and drip it into the hole (use the tip of a toothpick to work the resin down into the hole). Because of ICE Resin's self-healing properties, the hole may not be noticeable or appear as only a slight imperfection when it dries.

If your surface wasn't level or your bezel was lopsided (most often the case in rings or pre-made bezels already made into a linked bracelet) and it dried where one side is sloped, you can always mix up a small batch of resin, re-level your piece and drip more on top to even it out.

If you don't like your imagery and want to try again, sand down your dried resin with sandpaper. If you have a lot to remove, use a coarser 320 grit or less to remove, a finer 600 grit.

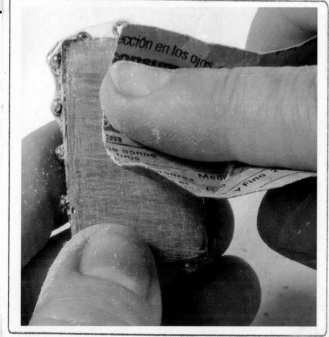

Your bezel will become scratched and opaque. It's OK. Layer the new image, mix a new batch of resin and drip more into the bezel or "paint" on a sealer coat. The scratches will disappear and the bezel will turn crystal clear. Seriously, it's magic before your eyes.

If you make a mistake you consider beyond repair and you feel you absolutely must preserve the bezel, there is a methylene chloride-based solvent called Attack™ that dissolves cured epoxy resin. The can carries hazardous health warnings, so please carefully read the information on the back label before using.

The most important thing to remember if you return to your studio to find a less-than-perfect bezel is to not despair. Remember these words of wisdom; You didn't make a mistake as long as you fix it before anyone can see it. Figure out which method is best for the situation: File it, sand it, scrape it or drill it and then re-pour new ICE Resin®.

Je tiens à vot
vous nous avez
S.t Geages. P.t
Recevez

French Journal
Susan Lenart Kazmer

Par Avarice
Susan Lenart Kazmer

I *Espree*
Susan Lenart Kazmer

A FINAL NOTE

As you can see by the previous chapters, ICE Resin® truly is an innovative product. Combined with all the incredible techniques Susan has developed over the past decade, there seems to be an unlimited amount of art-making potential.

From easy photo jewelry to advanced three-dimensional castings, you now have the basic techniques to begin your journey into this new art medium.

It's your turn, art voyager, to take what you've learned here and fly. Try the techniques and use the inspirational works of art from Susan, myself and the amazing Creative Team to make each piece of art you create your own. It's my sincere hope this book "resinated" with you as clearly as ICE Resin® has with me.

Follow Your Dreams and Soar, Jen Cushman
Prayer Box (left), Susan Lenart Kazmer

The Creative Team

KECIA DEVENEY

Originally from California, Kecia Deveney is a mixed media/jewelry artist /instructor/amateur photographer, residing at the Jersey Shore. Drawing inspiration from her life experiences as the mother of a severely disabled child, she channels that energy into learning and creating art. Experimenting with "reclaimed discardia" results in many unique pieces of storytelling art. She's been teaching at art retreats around the country and in her home studio for the past three years. Her goal as a teacher is to support, motivate and inspire others. Her work has been published in *Belle Armoire Jewelry*, *Altered Couture* and *Boho* Magazine. An active blogger, see more of Kecia at www.lemoncholys.blogspot.com

DERYN MENTOCK

With a strong passion for jewelry design, Deryn Mentock enjoys gathering unique, worn and well-loved finds, vintage religious pieces and semi-precious stones, as well as her own one-of-a-kind handmade elements, combining them in unexpected ways. Each composition, infused with color and texture, reveals an intuitive message of faith conveyed through the artist's hands. She travels to teach nationally, in addition to teaching online, and is committed to offering her students instruction in technique, as well as design and the creative process. Her work has been featured in numerous books and publications, including *Somerset Studio*, *Step by Step Wire Jewelry*, *Belle Armoire Jewelry*, *Handcrafted Jewelry* and many more. See more of her work at http://something-sublime.typead.com

KRISTEN ROBINSON

Kristen Robinson is on the artistic journey of her life, one she compares to dancing through the pages of a history book. With a love of all things from the past and the stories locked within them, she is drawn to many different forms of art from jewelry and textiles to painting and collage. Kristen's first book, *Tales of Adornment* is available this summer through North Light. She has expanded her teaching schedule to include on line courses (available through her blog). In addi-

Artist for *Somerset Studio* Magazine as well as a Bonne Vivante for *Somerset Life* Magazine. As a nationally known instructor and Artist she is truly finding great joy in sharing her journey with others. See more of Kristen at http://kristenrobinson.typepad.com

art dog DaeTzi in her new hometown of Santa Fe, NM. See her website at http://www.rsalley.com/jane/

BARBE SAINT JOHN

Mixed Media Artist Barbe Saint John has been creating all her life in one form or another. Like a modern-day alchemist, she's drawn to taking all things old, broken, forgotten, unusual and aged and melding them into one-of-kind pieces with a story all their own. Barbe's stash of jewelry and art-making supplies are reminiscent of a Victorian-era Cabinet of Curiosities. Numerous unique objects of a questionable past are at home here such as various bits of preserved flora and fauna, antique anatomy books, tiny bones, bits of old glass, antique medals and religious charms, vintage mother of pearl buckles, and even small antique sterling salt and pepper shakers. She has been featured in such magazines as *Belle Armoire*, *Jewelry Affaire*, and *Belle Armoire Jewelry*. Her jewelry and artwork can be found at boutiques and galleries across the country as well as online. See her website www.barbesaintjohn.com

JANE SALLEY

Known for her bold and whimsical style, Jane Salley has been creating art for as long as she can remember. At an early age she was fascinated by fashion, decorating and jewelry. In

recent years Jane has been following her passion to create beautiful things. Returning to her love of personal adornment she became a Precious Metal Clay instructor, receiving her PMC Certification under Master Jeweler Tim McCreight. Her PMC creations were recently exhibited at the Riverside Art Museum in Riverside, California. While her main focus these days is jewelry, her fashions can be seen in *Altered Couture, Haute Handbags* and *Sew* Somerset Magazines. Jane also enjoys teaching art to others and fanning the creative spark she believes is in everyone. Jane shares her creative live with her husband, Richard, and her

Resources

The products used in this book, including bezels, wire, chain, findings, beads, gears, fibers, molding putty and ICE Resin® are available at ICE Resin Susan Lenart Kazmer (www.ICEResin.com) and through her new company SLK Art Mechanic (www.slkartmechanic.com), as well as various independent and chain craft stores across the country. For a list of retailers of Susan's products, please see the company's ICE Resin website at www.ICEResin.com.

Other charms and beads, such as the small sparrow natural brass charm in Jen's "Follow Your Dreams and Soar" bracelet are from Vintaj (www.Vintaj.com). The company's beautiful charms are found at independent bead stores throughout the U.S.

Images used in Jen's Cuff, Wings and Things bracelet and Let Nature Lead the Way necklace are courtesy of ART chix Studio (www.artchixstudio.com). ART Chix has a lovely range of mixed media collage sheets available in paper form and instant download on its website. They have a generous "Angel Policy" for their images. I highly recommend this artist-based company.

The step-out photos in Chapter 3: Embedding and Inclusions are from Printmaker and Artist Denise Kester's piece "Raven Dream." She sells collage packs of her work at art fairs. To learn more, visit her website www.drawingonthedream.com

A note on images and copyright: Please respect artist's copyrights. Many people believe that if they take an original image and alter it that the image is no longer subject to copyright laws. This is a fallacy. More and more artists are making their images available for purchase on their Etsy and other individual store sites. If you plan to publish or sell your work, inquire about the artist's copyright policies before you create artwork using their images, even if you purchased them. Many mixed media online websites and rubber stamp companies offer generous "Angel Policies," which often give you rights to use the images as long as you credit appropriately.

Wings and Things, Jen Cushman